Cyclist BikeList

Cyclist BikeList
The Book for Every Rider

Laura Robinson

Illustrated by **Ramón K. Pérez**

Tundra Books

Published in Canada by Tundra Books,
75 Sherbourne Street, Toronto, Ontario M5A 2P9

Published in the United States by Tundra Books of Northern New York,
P.O. Box 1030, Plattsburgh, New York 12901

Library of Congress Control Number: 2008903004

Library and Archives Canada Cataloguing in Publication
Robinson, Laura
Cyclist bikelist : the book for every rider / Laura Robinson ; Ramón
Pérez, illustrator.
Includes index.
ISBN 978-0-88776-784-5
1. Bicycles–Juvenile literature. 2. Cycling–Juvenile literature.
I. Pérez, Ramón. II. Title. III. Title: Cyclist bikelist.
GV1043.5.R625 2010   j796.6   C2008-901809-5

We acknowledge the financial support of the Government of Canada through
the Book Publishing Industry Development Program (BPIDP) and that of
the Government of Ontario through the Ontario Media Development
Corporation's Ontario Book Initiative. We further acknowledge the support
of the Canada Council for the Arts and the Ontario Arts Council
for our publishing program.

ONTARIO ARTS COUNCIL
CONSEIL DES ARTS DE L'ONTARIO

Stock photography on pages 6-7 © Wellmony; page 18 © Anthony Hall; page 21 © Fjdelvalle;
page 23 © Pkruger. All used under license from Dreamstime.com

Design: Jennifer Lum
Printed in the United States of America

1 2 3 4 5 6   15 14 13 12 11 10

This book is dedicated to Karen Strong —one of the greatest cyclists ever.

ACKNOWLEDGMENTS

Many thanks to the following cyclists: Greg and David Robinson, brothers with whom I still ride and who know so much about the bicycle; Shane Jolley, Sean Laporte, and Tom English of Jolley's Alternative Wheels; Brett Martin of Martin's Cycles; the late Matt Terry, founder of the Saugeen Shores BMX Club; Barbara Wentworth, long-time cycling advocate extraordinaire; the many people over the years who taught me so much about how to really ride a bike; my agent, Hilary McMahon; editor Heather Sangster; James Genge for the title; and the very wonderful Kathy Lowinger of Tundra Books. Special thanks to Shania Squires for her editorial comments.

Finally, thank you to John Cameron, with whom I will ride to the ends of the earth.

CONTENTS

BECOMING A CYCLIST

I remember the April day when I fell in love with cycling. My brother and I took off on our bikes to celebrate the end of winter by riding farther than our mother would have allowed – had she known what we were up to.

Our route took us beyond our small Ontario town to a conservation area along the Niagara Escarpment. My brother was twelve, and I had just turned fourteen. In a way, we were cycling out of our childhoods.

When we arrived at the park, we ate every crumb of our packed lunch, drank as much water as possible, took a quick tour, and then headed home, flying with the wind at our backs. Round-trip, we cycled 37 miles (60 km) – our first real bike tour.

Upon our return, our mother's watchful eye detected our slightly glazed expressions – we were really tired but really happy. She knew we hadn't spent the day in school. Our faces were too tanned, our noses too runny, and my hair was a wind-blown mess. We were in trouble, but she still gave us three helpings each at dinner.

Soon after, my brother and I joined a cycling club. Our summer was spent soaring on two wheels as our bodies strengthened and our knowledge of the world around us deepened. No matter how early we started our ride, farmers were already working their land. It was they who fed us.

When I rode my bike, I wasn't a girl

who was expected not to have opinions –
I was a cyclist going as fast as I could,
sprinting against the boys to see who
could reach the crest of the hill first.

I was free.

Eventually I competed in cycling
across North America. After I hung up
my racing wheels, I toured half the globe
by bike. I work as a journalist, reporting
on cycling at the Olympics, and as a
coach of the Anishinaabe Racers of the
Chippewa of Nawash First Nation, near
Georgian Bay, Ontario. My brother is still
one of my favorite cycling partners.

You may have felt like we did that day
– when there was no difference between
us and the wind. Or maybe you've pedaled
along a bike path near water, cooling down
on a summer afternoon. Perhaps you've
cycled through your neighborhood, exploring a maze of alleyways with your
friends. Whatever the moment, spending
the rest of your life riding your bicycle
seemed like the best idea you ever had.

Whether you want to be a road racer,
tackling the legendary Alps in the Tour de
France, or know that cycling will help keep
you healthy and environmentally friendly,
you will realize that something about you
has changed. You aren't just making yourself
independent from your parental taxi service;
you aren't just someone who happens to
own a bicycle: *You are a Cyclist.*

1 The First Bicycles

No matter what scientists measure – the latest aerodynamic car or space-age jet, the stealthiest animal or sleekest fish – none match the bicycle for efficiency. When you consider the ratio of energy spent to distance traveled, there is no better way to get around than by bicycle. How brilliant the inventors of this two-wheeled engineering masterpiece were to imagine such an amazing machine into existence.

The bicycle has humble beginnings:

1817: Depending on who is telling the story, either Baron de Drais (according to the French) or Baron von Drais (according to the Austrians) was the inventor of the Draisienne (or Draisine), a wooden device with two wheels and handlebars. Also known as the hobby horse, push

Draisienne

Salvo

bike, or walking machine, the Draisienne looked like today's bicycle – without pedals! You powered the bike by pushing your feet against the ground. The Draisienne worked well for the baron, who rode along flat, manicured gardens, but not so well for everyone else on bumpy cobblestone roads.

1865: Pierre Lallemont of Paris claimed to invent the velocipede, or "fast foot," with a heavy steel frame, solid wooden wheels, and iron tires – so did carriage repairman Ernest Michaux of the United States. Both men added pedals to the front wheel, which allowed for riding on bumpy roads. The velocipede quickly became know as the Boneshaker.

1869: John Reynolds and John Mays replaced the bike's solid wooden wheels with wooden rims and wire spokes. Solid rubber tires were added, and heavy metals were used in the wheels. British cyclists called this bicycle the penny-farthing because its large front wheel resembled their penny.

1872: Through advances in metallurgy (stronger, lighter steel) and engineering (adding ball bearings inside moving

Penny-Farthing, later known as the Ariel

Velocipede

Rover (a.k.a. Safety)

parts to improve their "rolling ability"), the penny-farthing evolved into the Ariel – said to be the first real bicycle – created by James Starley of Starley & Co. in Coventry, England. By 1880, the Ariel was popular along the U.S. northeastern seaboard and as far west as Chicago and Indianapolis. It was also called the ordinary bicycle because the huge front wheel looked ordinary to people while same-size wheels on later bicycle designs were considered extraordinary.

1876: James Starley also built the first two-seat tricycle, the Salvo, which quickly became popular because it was more convenient and accessible than a horse carriage.

1884: Welding two penny-farthings together, M.D. Rucker created the first tandem bike. By the turn of the century, tandems had become fast, efficient bikes, great for courting (what dating was called back then).

1885: John Kemp Starley, James Starley's nephew, added a chain drive to the bicycle, allowing the wheels to be the same size, and the Rover was born. Its new design, with the rider sitting closer to the ground, also earned it the name "safety." Women in skirts were able to ride the safety, which increased sales immensely.

1887: When Scottish veterinarian John Boyd Dunlop wanted to make his son's

tricycle easier to ride, he developed a thin rubber tire that held air – not only inventing the pneumatic tire but also, finally, creating a truly comfortable bicycle. Cycling was now a pleasant pastime, a fast and exciting sport, and a means of transportation that more people could afford (though only the middle class rode until bicycles could be mass-produced).

1897: Smith & Starley Co. was joined by Raleigh Bikes and many other British and U.S. manufacturers in the production of bicycles with names such as the Victor, the Rambler, the Crescent, and the Columbia.

From the late nineteenth century until the 1920s, bicycles took Europe and North America by storm. They didn't need to be cared for and fed like horses; they were fun, promoted good health, and made it easy to leave home and explore a bigger world. It took smart people thinking about how wheels turned, how bodies worked, and how wonderful it was to see the world from a bicycle saddle to make cycling so fantastic. Today, there are more than one billion of these two-wheeled engineering masterpieces in use around the world.

Bicycle Parts

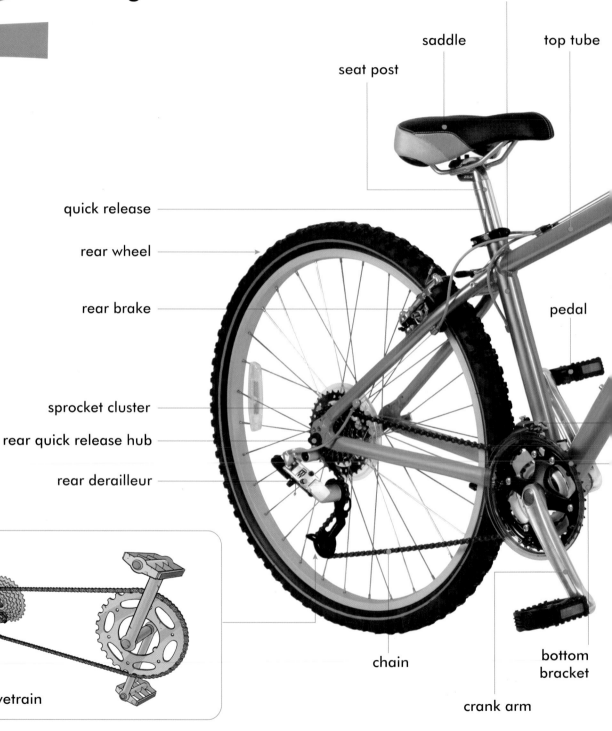

seat tube

saddle

top tube

seat post

seat post

quick release

rear wheel

rear brake

pedal

sprocket cluster

rear quick release hub

rear derailleur

chain

bottom bracket

crank arm

drivetrain

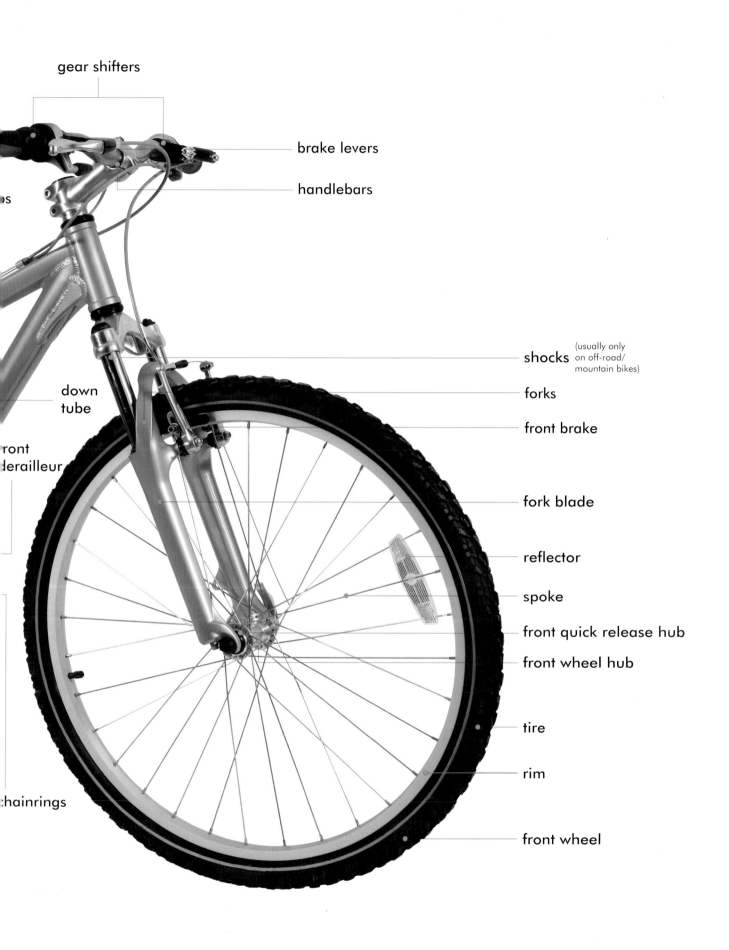

gear shifters

brake levers

handlebars

os

down
tube

ront
derailleur

chainrings

shocks (usually only
on off-road/
mountain bikes)

forks

front brake

fork blade

reflector

spoke

front quick release hub

front wheel hub

tire

rim

front wheel

How Does a Bike Work?

WHEELS

Let's start with why it's a bicycle in the first place: wheels. A bike has more than just two of them. The rear derailleur has two pulleys – which are small, light wheels – that allow the chain to flow freely when gears change. Your chain also runs over chainrings at the front and sprockets at the back – more little wheels.

BIKE WHEELS

	Road	Hybrid	Off-Road (Mountain Bike)	BMX
Rims	Rim diameter with tire on: 28 in. (700 mm). Shallow rim, made of aluminum/alloys. single-wall	Rim diameter with tire on: 28 in. (700 mm) and up, as hybrid tires can be wider and knobbier than road tires. Rim is wider, made of aluminum/alloys.	Rim diameter with tire: 24 in. (610 mm) and up, depending on tire knobbie-ness. Double-walled rim for punishment of trail riding, made of aluminum/alloy/steel. double-wall	Large variety of wheels: for track racing, general riding; wheels 23 in. (570 m) diameter, increases with knobbier tires. Rim usually made of steel for added strength. Cruiser Class: 24 in. (610 mm).
Spokes	stainless steel or carbon fiber	stainless steel	stainless steel	stainless steel
Hubs	light alloy	alloy	alloy	alloy
Tires	Lightweight, high pressure, narrow, very tight fit on rim, removal very difficult, even with tire irons. Extra tube is rolled up under saddle with tire irons and patch kit. Pump should always be on bike so punctures can be fixed "on the road."	High to medium pressure, tires wider and knobbier than road tires, and much easier to remove.	Medium to low pressure, aggressive tread for good grip, tires come off rim easily once deflated. Downhill mountain bike wheels: extra knobby tires.	High to medium pressure, aggressive tires for dirt track. Slick road tires are smooth, only for racing trails. "Micro-knobbies" for novice trails.

DRIVETRAIN

When powered by legs and feet, the drivetrain is the mechanism running the bike. It includes pedals, which rotate crank arms that connect to the bottom bracket. Attached to the crank arm may be one or more chainrings that drive the chain, which rotates the rear wheel via the rear sprockets (cassette or freewheel).

GEARING RATIO

Gearing ratios were the driving force behind the development of the safety bike, with its same-size wheels and drivetrain to turn the rear wheel. A safety bike's drivetrain includes a gear at the pedals (driven by the pedals) and a gear at the rear wheel (driving the rear wheel); both are connected by a chain. If different-circumference gears are used on either end of the drivetrain, one revolution of the pedals could turn the rear wheel multiple times. This is accomplished by having a large gear at the pedals and a small gear at the rear wheel.

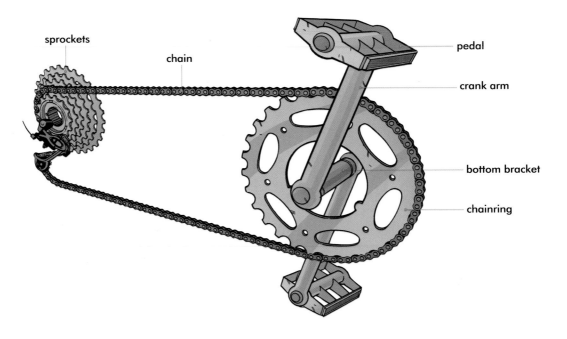

sprockets

chain

pedal

crank arm

bottom bracket

chainring

NATURAL FUEL
The energy provided by the circular turning of legs allows the ball of your foot to apply force to the pedals, which the drivetrain converts into a forward action as the chain moves along the rear sprockets and the front chainrings. Because the cogs are connected to the hub, the movement turns the hub, which turns the back wheel, while the rest of the bicycle and the cyclist's body transfer that energy to move the bicycle forward. (Whew!)

The ratio of the circumferences of gears is called the gear ratio. This ratio determines how many rotations the rear wheel makes for each pedal revolution. With the right gear ratio, one pedal revolution on a safety bike could turn the rear wheel enough times to make the bike travel farther than one revolution of the large front wheel on a penny-farthing. Gear ratios allowed safety bikes to produce the same speed as "high wheelers" without worrying about "taking a header," hence the "safety" name.

Do the Math

How did inventors figure out what size wheels and gear ratios were needed so the safety bike would outperform the high wheeler? Math.

If you divide the number of teeth on the front gear by the number of teeth on the rear gear, then multiple the result by the diameter of the wheel, you come up with a number. This number equals the distance the bike travels during one pedal revolution. You've just figured out gear inches.

But bike builders didn't stop there. Because gears on safety bikes were relatively small, why not install multiple gears, use both rear and front derailleurs to move the chain from gear to gear, and have multiple gear ratios? Multiple gear ratios allow cyclists to turn the pedals at a relatively constant rate, achieving different speeds by changing gears and maintaining fairly constant speed over hilly terrain. Voilá – the bicycle as we know it had arrived. The terms *7-speed*, *8-speed*, and *10-speed* refer to the number of gears in the rear cluster of sprockets. The terms *single*, *double*, and *triple* refer to the number of gears (chainrings) at the pedals.

GEAR INCHES TABLE

Efficient gear ratios are important for reducing strain on your knees and fine-tuning your speed and endurance – especially if you're competing. A big ratio (48 teeth on front chainring, 14 on rear) is hard to pedal but will travel farthest with one pedal revolution (96 inches [8 feet], or 244 cm [2.5 m])—it's for downhills and tailwinds. For climbing and headwinds, use smaller numbers on the front and bigger numbers on the rear. You won't go as far per pedal revolution, but it'll be easier to do.

26-Inch (66 cm) Wheel*
Rear gear tooth values = Number of teeth on rear hub cog

Front gear tooth values = Number of teeth on front chainrings

	14	15	16	17	18	19	20	21	22	23	24	25	26
48	96.0	89.6	84.0	79.0	74.6	70.7	67.2	64.0	61.0	58.4	56.0	53.7	51.6
47	94.0	87.7	82.2	77.4	73.1	69.2	65.8	62.6	59.8	57.2	54.8	52.6	50.6
46	92.0	85.8	80.5	75.7	71.5	67.7	64.3	61.3	58.5	56.0	53.6	51.5	49.5
45	90.0	84.0	78.7	74.1	70.0	66.3	63.0	60.0	57.2	54.7	52.5	50.4	48.4
44	88.0	82.1	77.0	72.4	68.4	64.8	61.6	58.6	56.0	53.5	51.3	49.2	47.3
43	86.0	80.2	75.2	70.8	66.8	63.3	60.1	57.3	54.7	52.3	50.1	48.1	46.3
42	84.0	78.3	73.5	69.1	65.3	61.8	58.8	56.0	53.4	51.1	49.0	47.0	45.2
41	82.0	76.5	71.7	67.5	63.7	60.4	57.3	54.6	52.1	49.9	47.8	45.9	44.1
40	80.0	74.6	70.0	65.8	62.2	58.9	56.0	53.3	50.9	48.6	46.6	44.8	43.0
39	78.0	72.8	68.2	64.2	60.6	57.4	54.6	52.0	49.6	47.4	45.5	43.6	42.0
38	76.0	70.9	66.5	62.5	59.1	56.0	53.1	50.6	48.3	46.2	44.3	42.5	40.9
37	74.0	69.0	64.7	60.9	57.5	54.5	51.8	49.3	47.0	45.0	43.1	41.4	39.8
36	72.0	67.2	63.0	59.2	56.0	53.0	50.4	48.0	45.8	43.8	42.0	40.3	38.7
35	70.0	65.3	61.2	57.6	54.4	51.5	49.0	46.6	44.5	42.6	40.8	39.1	37.6
34	68.0	63.4	59.5	56.0	52.8	50.1	47.6	45.3	43.2	41.3	39.6	38.0	36.6
33	66.0	61.6	57.7	54.3	51.3	48.6	46.1	44.0	42.0	40.1	38.5	36.9	35.5
32	64.0	59.7	56.0	52.7	49.7	47.1	44.8	42.6	40.7	38.9	37.3	35.8	34.4
31	62.0	57.8	54.2	51.0	48.2	45.6	43.4	41.3	39.4	37.7	36.1	34.7	33.3
30	60.0	56.0	52.5	49.4	46.6	44.2	42.0	40.0	38.1	36.5	35.0	33.6	32.3
29	58.0	54.1	50.7	47.7	45.2	42.7	40.6	38.6	36.9	35.3	33.8	32.4	31.2
28	56.0	52.2	49.0	46.1	43.5	41.2	39.1	37.3	35.6	34.0	32.6	31.3	30.1
27	54.0	50.4	47.2	44.4	42.0	39.7	37.8	36.0	34.3	32.8	31.5	30.2	29.0
26	52.0	48.5	45.5	42.8	40.4	38.3	36.4	34.6	33.0	31.6	30.3	29.1	28.0

* BMX bikes have single gears, varying widely depending on rider's ability/course profile. Riders experiment with different ratios for fun and for advantage in races.

GEARS

	Road	Hybrid	Off-Road (Mountain Bike)	BMX
Drive-train	Newer bikes: 10-speed doubles. Older models: 9-, 8-, and 7-speed doubles. For touring, front chainrings are frequently triples.	Newer bikes: 10-speed triples. Older models: 9-, 8-, and 7-speed triples.	Newer bikes: 10-speed triples. Older models: 9- and 8-speed triples.	All single speed, many ratios used by wrenching rear sprocket off and replacing with different amount of teeth.

Use this easy equation to find out the total amount of gears you have:
Number of rings on front chainring x Number of sprockets on back

HANDLEBARS, BRAKES, AND PEDALS

	Road	Hybrid	Off-Road (Mountain Bike)	BMX
Handle-bars	"Drop" or "Aero" with some bars ergonomically formed. Light aluminum/alloys/carbon fiber.	"Drop" or flat; flat may be raised. Light aluminum/alloys/carbon fiber.	Flat or raised. Light aluminum/alloys/carbon fiber.	Rise up slightly for young riders. Older, experienced riders have up to a 7-in. (18-cm) rise with crossbar for added strength. Widths vary depending on rider preference. Usually light steel.
Brakes	Dual-pivot, side-pull rim brakes. Light aluminum alloys.	Dual-pivot, side-pull rim brakes; linear pull/V-brakes; or disk brakes. Light aluminum alloys.	Linear pull/V-brakes or disk brakes. Light aluminum alloys.	Freestyle U/dual-pivot, side-pull rim brakes on front, back. Racers use single linear-pull on rear. Light aluminum alloys.
Pedals	Clipless single-sided. Aluminum alloys, titanium, carbon fiber.	Clipless double-sided or platform. Aluminum alloys, titanium, carbon fiber.	Clipless double-sided or platform. Aluminum alloys, titanium, carbon fiber.	Platform. Aluminum alloys, steel. Some road clipless pedals.

FRAMES

Road Bike:

- Front wheel close to down tube.
- Rear wheel close to seat tube.
- High-tech, lightweight materials for frame.
- Steep, tight angles make short wheel base. (Wheel base = distance between rear stays, where wheel's hub attaches to bike, and end of front forks, where front hub attaches to bike: hub to hub).

Hybrid Bike:

- Medium amount of space between front wheel/down tube.
- Medium amount of space between seat tube/rear wheel.
- Most often aluminum or steel frame.

Off-Road (Mountain) Bike:

- Large space between front wheel/down tube.
- Lots of space between seat tube/rear wheel.
- Wider, more relaxed angles make long wheel base.
- Most often aluminum or steel frame.

BMX Bikes:

RACE BIKES:

- Size of bike measured by length of top tube. Small bikes categorized as "micro" and "mini." Older kids go "Pro," "Pro-Excel," "Extra, Extra," and even "Triple Extra" for adults.
- Chromoly, aluminum, or carbon fiber frame.

FREESTYLE BIKE:

A freestyle bike is for aggressive street riding and to "catch air" and "get vertical" at skate parks on half-pipes. It's a sub-group of BMX competition at events like X Games. Super-sturdy construction is a higher priority than lightweight. The wheels are usually "mag" – heavy-duty nylon with 48-wire spokes. Tires are 20 x 2.125 inches (51 x 5.4 cm) or wider, with fairly smooth treads because they're predominantly pavement pounders. Axle pegs are often included (riders use them for stunts). It has a five-piece handlebar and a seat with a hard plastic edge so if the bike drops, the seat stays intact. It also comes with front and rear brakes and "knurling" on the tubing and top bar of the handlebar to prevent slipping if/when you stand on them. The front cable is routed through a "rotor" or "detangler," allowing handlebars to spin completely around without tangling the brake cables.

DIRT JUMPER:

As the name suggests, a dirt jumper is designed to take flight. It bridges the wide gap between BMX and freestyle (beefier than the former, lighter than the latter). It usually doesn't have front brakes, and its brawny wheels normally have 36 rugged 13-gauge spokes rather than freestyle's 48 spokes. Occasionally, it is equipped with 24-inch (61-cm) wheels – and is an excellent choice for larger riders.

FLATLAND BIKE:

With its little, low-slung wedgie seat – or no seat at all – the flatland is in its own weird category. This bike isn't about going fast – it's about balancing, as if it was a mobile climbing apparatus for gymnasts. Yes, bike gymnastics. Trials riders hop up on railings, ride down, then flip around on a set of stairs, hopping back to the top of the railing – whatever. A flatland needs really good brakes. Wheel size varies from 20 to 26 inches (51 to 66 cm), and gear ratio is 1:1. It can be ridden like a unicycle; if you pedal backward, you go backward. Not a terribly practical way to get to anywhere on time.

4 Choosing a Bike

You've outgrown your first bike, so what next? With a variety of road bikes, BMX and freestyle bikes, downhill bikes, track bikes, off-road (mountain) bikes, and cruisers – in different colors, with many kinds of gears, tires, handlebars, you name it – how do you choose?

Road bikes are for road racing (best

started around age fourteen); they can only be ridden on paved surfaces and cost a fortune. BMX and freestyle bikes are used at special tracks. BMX tracks are short racecourses (1,000 to 2,000 feet, or 300 to 600 m) with hills and jumps. Freestyle parks have rock ledges, picnic tables, teeter-totters – everyday items and specially built devices that cyclists balance on, jump over, catwalk (balancing on one wheel), or dive through. Freestyle riding involves certain risks. You'll have to develop a great deal of skill. And freestyle bikes aren't very practical for transportation, so you might end up needing *two* bikes!

Track bikes are not sold in bike stores. They have to be specially made, with no gears or brakes! The bike's single speed is called a "fixed wheel," which means once you start pedaling, the pedals keep turning – you can't coast. The sprocket is screwed directly on the hub of the wheel and then everything is secured by a lockring. If you want to change gears, you have to replace the sprocket with one that has a different number of teeth. Track cyclists slow down by using their leg muscles to reduce the pedaling action. Track bikes are ridden mostly in velodromes (French for "bicycle racecourse") – if you watched the Olympics, you saw track cyclists practically defying gravity as

they flew around a wooden track with really steep banking. It takes a lot of time and skill to become a good track cyclist: you have to create enough speed to build up the necessary centrifugal force to keep you from sliding down the banking. Can you imagine what would happen if you stopped suddenly at a 45-degree angle? You'd slide right down to the bottom of the track, or "the apron." That would hurt!

So before you buy a bike, think about what you want and need. Where will you ride? A mountain bike with dual suspension and dirt-eating tires isn't efficient on pavement. If you long for those gnarly trails in the park, forget road bikes and hybrids. Rocks, stumps, and exposed roots will quickly turn them into pretzels. Ask your friends if they have a bike they like. Try out other kids' bikes at school and in your neighborhood, but remember to wear your helmet.

For kids who are still growing, who like riding on roads and some easy off-roading, and who don't want to spend a lot of money for a bike that won't fit in a year or two, hybrids are perfect. They combine the best of lightweight road bikes and durable mountain bikes. You can soar along on roads, but if you also want to ride on hard-packed dirt trails, this is the bike for you.

COMPARING BIKE STYLES
Road Bike

FRAME: The steep angles on a road bike create a very efficient ride, which ensures that all energy translates to speed. But this stiff bike is also unforgiving, sending every little bump into your hands and crotch. A road bike demands good cycling skills on corners and quick turns. Because the front wheel is so close to the bike's frame, when a pedal is in its most forward position your foot can hit the wheel when taking a corner. With the light, stiff tubing comes really skinny wheels and tires with minimal treads

that can be demolished by the average pothole, so choose your terrain wisely.

GEARS: Designed to go fast with little effort, a road bike should have 14 to 20 gears. Newer models usually include a 9- or 10-gear sprocket cluster (also known as a cassette or freewheel) on the rear wheel and only two chainrings on the front wheel. Sprockets, cassettes, and freewheels are all the same thing: the teethed circles connected to the rear wheel. They determine your gear ratio (see page 11), which is directly related to the distance you cover, in inches, every time you pedal one complete revolution. Chainrings are the large circles that the crank arms are attached to (the crank arms attach the pedals to the bike).

BRAKES: A road bike usually has side-pull (caliper) brakes with a cable attached to one side. The cable runs through an adjusting sleeve and lockring, then through an area with a tiny quick-release lever that sticks out, attached to an anchor bolt. When you flip the quick-release lever up and down, the brake pads on either side of the rim move. It's very convenient when taking wheels on and off, as a flick of the quick release slides the brake pads apart and an inflated tire can fit through.

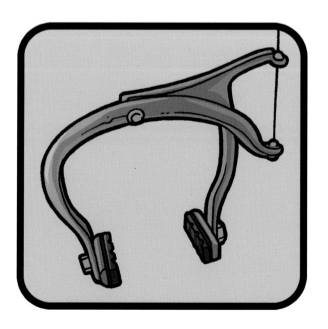

A TRUE STORY

Bike-shop mechanics may let you watch a pro true a wheel and try it for yourself. Truing wheels is an art and science that takes lots of practice. (Work on used wheels until you get the hang of it. There are endless supplies of trashed wheels.) Turn an old pair of forks upside down and anchor them on a table so the wheel sits in them. Then anchor a piece of chalk so as the wheel turns in the forks, you can see where the rim rubs against the chalk, which is where you start loosening and tightening spokes. To loosen and tighten, you need a spoke key, which you can buy at a bike shop.

If you hit an object that makes your wheel wobble and go "out of true," it will rub against the brakes, making pedaling difficult. Pulling the quick-release brake lever out pulls the brake pads away from the rim until you can have your wheel trued or replaced.

FORKS: Fork "rake" is one of the most important differences among road bikes, hybrids, and mountain bikes. It is the perpendicular distance from the steering axis to the center of the front wheel and affects the steering and turning capacity of a bike – basically how it handles. Road forks have a steep rake, which means that the blades of

CHANGING GEARS

Practice changing gears in a safe area. The chain must be moving, which means you must pedal and change gears at the same time. Don't use such a small gear that you barely move with each pedal revolution and start bouncing in the saddle. Don't use such a big gear that you work too hard. Feel the difference between gears, and look down at your chainring and rear sprocket to see what gears you are in. Find your rhythm – the right gear and a smooth pedal revolution that doesn't take all your strength. When you are still growing, you can do damage to your knees if gears are too big. As you get older and ride more, you will be able to push bigger gears. Remember, the pros always start the season in small gears, putting in thousands of miles "spinning" easier gears before using the "big ring." A smooth spinning action is essential to good riding.

each fork are almost straight, keeping the front wheel very close to the frame – nearly hitting it. Like the steep frame angles, this allows the bike to move forward efficiently but with your body absorbing every bump.

OTHER PARTS TO CONSIDER: A road bike has dropped handlebars – not great for city riding. When you're "on the drops,"

you are quite low, yet you need to be fairly upright in city traffic. Also, the pedals on a road bike are very small and have a clasp that fastens to cleats on cycling shoes. This gives 360 degrees of power through one pedal revolution, but your shoes are locked in and you have to twist your foot to disengage from the pedals, which can be tricky if you have to dismount quickly. Excellent cycling skills are necessary for this. Finally, a road bike can cost thousands of dollars – it's best to wait until you're older and committed to racing before you buy this style of bike.

Off-Road (Mountain) Bike

FRAME: Compared to both a road bike and a hybrid, an off-road (mountain) bike has much more relaxed angles in its frame design. You're going to hit rocks and roots and jump a bit, so the bike frame needs to be able to absorb jarring shocks and not transfer them through your arms, feet, and butt. Thicker tires with "knobbier" treads (called "knobbies") also help you maneuver comfortably along rough terrain.

GEARS: A mountain bike often has either 24, 27, or 30 gears, with the newer models including a 10-gear sprocket cluster on the rear wheel and 3 chainrings on the front

wheel. A large number of gears allows you to pedal at the same pace no matter what kind of terrain you're on. When mountain bikers ride up steep hills, they have to contend with rocks, dirt, roots, and narrow trails that cause lots of friction for tires. The best way to maneuver is to put the bike in a really small gear that's easy to pedal, usually called the "granny gear." A mountain bike's granny gear has fewer teeth than a hybrid's granny gear.

BRAKES: All good mountain bikes and plenty of hybrids now come with disk brakes, either hydraulic or mechanical. (Hydraulic brakes are for hardcore moun-tain bikers and require special tools and hydraulic fluid. You don't want to spill this stuff on the living-room carpet!)

Mechanical disk brakes are very cool because you pull in one direction with the brake cable and that pushes the brake pads in a 90-degree motion. This is possible be-cause of a ball-bearing action called a "ball and ramp mechanism" within the caliper that houses this part of the brake. It's like a car's emergency brake. When you pull on the brake lever at the handlebars, it pulls on the cable that runs down to another lever at the hub level where the brake is located.

With regular caliper brakes, the brake pads grab the wheel's rim. But think about the grime and grit the brake pads grind into your rims every time you use them, especially in the rain. Instead, imagine that the disk sitting on your wheel's hub is just like the wheel: calipers that sit on the disk's rim are what stop the bike. This mechanism is farther away from road debris, and because it operates at the axis of the wheel and not way out at the rim, it is a far more efficient location for brakes.

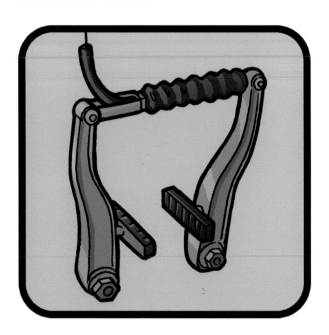

Older or less expensive mountain bikes have V-brakes, which use the same design as side-pull road brakes but are more durable and have at least twice the power. Check these brakes for spring the same way you would for hybrid brakes. They are very easy to loosen in order to take your wheels on and off, so get someone in the shop to show you how it's done. Practice until you get the hang of it.

Whether your bike has disk or V-brakes, if it has been assembled properly, the brake cables are lubricated. Lube allows for better cable movement within the housing and keeps water out, which rusts cables.

FORKS: For rougher off-roading, you need a mountain bike's suspension forks. These forks have shocks. Press down on the handlebars and the forks will have lots of play for jumping rocks and logs. Suspension forks will allow for adjustment, so tighten them while riding on roads, then

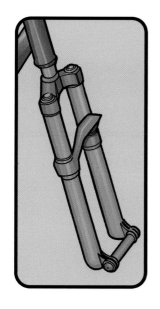

loosen for off-road riding. Don't worry about rear suspension. Unless you buy a really expensive bike (which you will grow out of anyway), rear suspension will break down constantly and add unnecessary weight.

RIMS: See Hybrid Rims.

Hybrid Bike

FRAME: A hybrid bike has angles similar to, but not as steep as, a road bike. Wheels aren't nearly as close to the frame, so your bike will have more spring, absorb more of the vibrations from bumpy roads, and be forgiving should you make small mistakes steering or cornering. A hybrid also has thicker tires with a visible tread pattern. Long-distance cycling – assuming that the bike is the right size, you and your saddle get along, and you choose the right handlebars – is fantastic on these

bikes, as is cruising your neighborhood and riding to school.

GEARS: A hybrid should have 21 to 30 gears. The newer models include a 9-or 10-gear sprocket cluster on the rear wheel and 3 chainrings on the front wheel, which give you more variety in gearing. The third chainring is a granny gear. For everyone who isn't Lance Armstrong, granny gears help to scale steep inclines. You won't break any speed records pedaling a granny gear, but on a hybrid you should be able to get up the steepest of the fairly smooth hills in your neighborhood.

BRAKES: See Off-Road Bike Brakes.

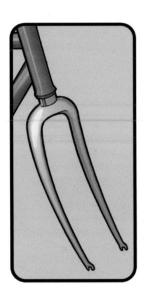

FORKS: Hybrid forks have a more relaxed angle than road forks (you can see a slight curve to the fork blade in the illustration), creating more distance between the front wheel and the frame. If you hit a bump, hybrid forks will allow the vibration to travel farther so by the time it reaches your body, it isn't so great. Still, these forks don't have enough give to go beyond gentle off-road trails.

RIMS: Another important feature of hybrid and mountain bikes is hidden by the tire, so ask bike-shop staff to show you the rim without the tire and tube. For trail riding, you need double-walled rims. Single-walled rims, on lower-priced bikes, will be destroyed the first time you jump an object and land hard, which is often the first day out. Not only will you need a brand-new wheel, you won't be riding until the bike is repaired. Double-walled rims have limits but will endure more abuse.

A Note on Quick Release
All three bikes should have quick-release wheels, though some bicycle manufacturers are now using nuts and bolts on front wheels because many people don't tighten quick releases properly, which can cause terrible accidents. Often bikes have quick-release mechanisms for seat posts, so if you lock your bike somewhere but are still worried about theft, you can take your seat with you. Mountain bikers change seat

height depending on terrain. On steep downhills, their weight is behind the seat, so it must be low enough for them to push themselves behind it and still reach the handlebars.

If you have to pack your bike in a box or trunk, a quick-release seat and wheels makes it easy, as your bike quickly strips down to wheels, frame, handlebars, and pedals. Now it will fit into the smallest of trunks. Don't forget your seat when you unload – unless you want to stand up for the whole ride. (BMX bikes don't have quick-release parts, so bring wrenches.)

Quick releases cost more than the nut and washers found on cheaper bikes, but you will love them. Riding with your saddle too high or too low is very un-comfortable and inefficient. You can adjust a quick-release saddle while waiting for a light to turn green. When on the saddle, the area from your toes to the ball of the foot should touch the ground. If you can stand flatfooted while on the saddle, the bike is too small. Saddles go up/down,

backward/forward, so consult bike-shop staff about how far the seat post can be raised for your growing body. (Mark it with tape so you know your seat post height next time your bike is apart.)

If you have quick-release wheels, it is easy to change from hybrid to mountain bike tires should you want to venture into different terrain. Read the side of the tires to find out how much air they can take. It is important to have the correct pressure or cycling becomes a huge effort. For trail riding, you often want less air in your tires. Riding over roots and rocks is easier on slightly soft tires. Carry a pump on your bike and a spare tube in a little pouch under the saddle for pumping up soft tires or changing punctured ones. Talk to bike-shop staff about various tire pressures.

There is a particular technique when tightening quick releases, and if you don't learn it, you could smash your teeth and forehead to smithereens.

Practice using the quick release on the front wheel with bike-shop staff.

SHOPPING FOR A BIKE STORE

If possible, look for a new bike with someone who really knows bicycles and knows what you need.

Choose a bike shop that offers a variety of quality bicycles, parts, and accessories, does repairs, and has friendly staff that can advise you on the best combination of equipment. Your bicycle should be tailored to suit you. Find the right place with the right people to do that.

Good bike-shop employees will make sure the bike fits you correctly and will allow you to take it for a test ride. They should also quiz you on your cycling needs: Riding to school? Off-road? Touring the Rockies? All these options require different bike features.

They'll advise you to return for adjustments. Bicycles need tune-ups and repairs; it's normal to adjust gear and brake cables once a new bike is broken in. Or you may need a shorter handlebar stem. Maybe the saddle is torturing you. Although you'll have to pay for any upgrades on bike parts or accessories, installation and adjustments in this initial time period should be free (depending on the warranty). Make sure this is noted on your sales receipt — and don't leave it in your pocket so it can go through the laundry. Start your own "bike file" at home and put the receipt in it.

SHOPPING FOR A BIKE

Sizing

To find out if a bike is your size, straddle the top tube. On road bikes, hybrids, and mountain bikes, there should be between 1 and 2 inches (2.5 and 5 cm) of clearance between you and the top tube. BMX and trick bikes will be much smaller, with up to 7 inches (18 cm) of clearance.

You must be able to reach the brake levers (which are attached and run parallel to the handlebars) and pedals easily, with your elbows relaxed and slightly bent. Sit on the saddle, have someone hold the bike steady, and place your feet on the pedals.

Ask someone to ride behind you and watch the muscles in your back (above your shorts line) as you pedal. If they move up and down (your back doesn't remain very level) and your head bobs, your saddle is too high.

With one leg positioning a pedal at 90 degrees to the ground, on your other leg you should be able to draw an imaginary line from about half an inch (1 cm) below the kneecap down through the middle of your foot. There should be a little flex in your knee. This leg position will allow for the best flow of power from your strong thigh and butt muscles to the ball of your foot, which then transfers the power to the pedal.

Cycle Smart, Cycle Safe

If you cycle in the city, you've jumped pot-holes and sewer grates and swerved around shards of glass, gutter garbage, skate-boarders, roller-bladers, dog-walkers, dog poop, and pedestrians who don't watch for traffic. You've ridden a safe distance from parked vehicles so you won't be "doored" by numbskulls opening doors before looking. Your eyes are mine sweepers, scanning for every encounter.

If you cycle in the country, you've had your share of dog chases and middle-finger waves from those who want you off the road. Your digestive system got used to bugs as they flew into your mouth, and it's only taken one bug to the eye, or gravel sprayed by a vehicle, to make sure you always wear sunglasses while cycling.

If you cycle in the suburbs, there are usually no bike lanes and sometimes no sidewalks. The roads in your neighborhood are not designed for cyclists. They have high curbs with right angles that prevent you from moving quickly to the right if need be.

No matter where you've cycled, you've likely been caught in torrential downpours far away from home. Rain has turned to snow, and your frozen hands have nearly become permanently clamped to the handlebars as you steer along slippery roads. You've forgotten your waterbottle on hot and humid days and wondered if you weren't going to become one of those dried-up milkweed pods on the roadside. You only do that once. As much fun as cycling is, to enjoy it fully you need to be prepared – for almost anything.

MUST-HAVE EQUIPMENT
Always Wear a Helmet

Have you ever dropped a watermelon and even though it's not far from the floor it splatters everywhere? Imagine that watermelon is your head and you'll understand why wearing a helmet is so important.

Your skull is the thickness of a stack of three pennies. That's all there is between your very valuable brain and the ground. Your brain sits inside the skull, surrounded by fluid. When you hit your head, your brain crashes up against the inside of your skull. It can bruise, swell, and bleed. Protect your head by always wearing a helmet and practicing safe cycling. Most provinces and states have helmet laws. Cyclists in British Columbia must wear helmets, as must children (under nineteen years of age) in Ontario. But don't wear a helmet because it's law – wear one to always protect your brain!

Look for a CSA- or SNELL-approved helmet. Don't buy secondhand helmets because if they've been hit or dropped, the Styrofoam liner won't absorb an impact very well. And if your helmet gets hit or is dropped, for instance, onto concrete, replace it even if it still looks okay.

Bike-shop staff can show you how to fit the helmet properly. Adjust the helmet at the back until it fits snugly on your head. Do up the straps so they make a V and meet just under your ear. The chin strap should be snug but not choking. You should be able to place two fingers between your eyebrow and your helmet.

If your helmet sits back too far, it won't cover your forehead. These days, there are plenty of cool helmets to choose from that are so light you'll forget you're wearing one. But don't go cycling without it!

All the Bells and Whistles

Traffic law requires that your bike be equipped with a front white light and a red rear light to improve your visibility on the road. Many snap on and off, so you can take them inside if you think others might like them too. A bell is also mandatory. In city traffic, pedestrians about to step into the curb lane in front of you without checking usually respond more quickly to a bell than a verbal warning. In rural areas, particularly in bear country, always carry "bear bells." Bears don't like a lot of noise and will normally disappear if they hear your clatter.

OBEY THE SIGNS

Under the law, you are considered a vehicle – with the same rights as motorized vehicles, so know your traffic signs and act accordingly.

Stop

Always stop, look, and give pedestrians the right of way. If possible, make eye contact with drivers too. A friendly nod goes a long way.

Yield

Yield means you have to let other traffic go first. You are "merging" with another stream of traffic. Exercise caution, as drivers tend to look for cars but not bikes.

Pedestrian Crossing

You can do serious damage to, or even kill, a pedestrian if you hit them while on your bike. If you end up on the sidewalk sometimes, be polite and walk your bike around people, especially the elderly and little kids.

Railway Crossing

Train tracks often cross at odd angles. Cross tracks at a right angle so your wheels don't slide, but only if there isn't any traffic. It's better to get off your bike at the shoulder and walk it over the tracks, especially if they are wet. Streetcar tracks can also be very slippery and at

funny angles. It's best to cross streetcar tracks like a pedestrian as well.

Road Narrows

This sign often appears before a bridge or construction area where traffic lanes disappear. Be careful and make sure there are no vehicles behind you at the same time as you see oncoming vehicles. This is another area to exercise caution in and get off the road and walk through.

No Cyclists Allowed or Cyclists Route

Pay attention to where you're allowed to ride. Cyclists are not allowed on big highways, and sometimes other really busy roads don't let them on. But more cities have routes that favor cyclists. Sometimes only cyclists can use certain streets at rush hour, or turn left and right on certain roads. Your city's cycling committee has maps that show safe bike routes.

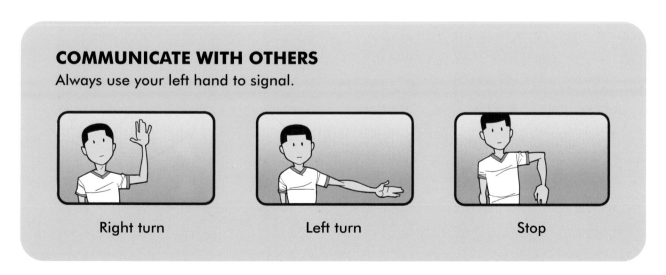

COMMUNICATE WITH OTHERS
Always use your left hand to signal.

Right turn   Left turn   Stop

Do's and Don'ts for a Safe Ride

- *Always ride in a straight line on the road's right side, with traffic flow.*

- *Don't ride too close to the curb.*
  - › Create space to move away should a car come too close on your left.
  - › Watch for car doors opening to your right and general debris that gets pushed into the bike lane.

- *Always ride defensively. Try to predict what drivers will do.*
  - › Intersections are potential dangers. Because you are a vehicle, you must stop at the stop sign. Check before entering an intersection, even if drivers have the stop sign. Drivers do "rolling stops" and begin moving before they look for cyclists, especially smaller ones. Others don't stop until well past the stop sign and can hit you if you are riding off the sidewalk. Many drivers don't think about sidewalk traffic.
  - › Watch for drivers turning right at intersections and ignoring you completely. They are breaking the law. Stop before the collision occurs, and *yell and use your bell.* If they get angry, remember you are in the right. If they get out of the car, quickly move to the sidewalk; yell for help. Most likely

there will be witnesses. Drivers cannot overtake another vehicle (you) just before an intersection and turn right while that vehicle (you) is going straight. They shouldn't even turn right at the same time you turn right. They should wait until you have turned safely, then make their turn.

- *Always do shoulder checks and signal correctly.*
  - › If you decide to turn left at a quiet, empty street, look behind your left shoulder. Is the coast clear? Should you slow down and wait for oncoming traffic to pass you by? These decisions are up to you. You may have to do several shoulder checks before you establish the right time to signal your turn.
  - › The next step is to *always* signal, even if there are no cars. It's automatic. If you find yourself signaling to a field of cows, who cares? Just keep doing it.
  - › As you signal, move left into the middle of your lane, but do not cross into the oncoming lane. *You must never ride in the oncoming lane.* Do another shoulder check. Is the coast still clear behind/in front of you? By now you should be at the intersection.
  - › Make your turn and remember to ride into the right lane of the new

road. You don't want to be cycling on the left side into oncoming vehicles. Practice this in areas that don't have much traffic until you can confidently turn.

Unless you are on a street without traffic, don't even try a left turn from a vehicle lane. Pull over to the curb, get off your bike, and do a pedestrian crossing either at crosswalks, stop signs, intersections, or a set of lights.

- *If temperatures are at zero or below, don't go cycling.*
  › If there is any water on the road, it will freeze; ice is extremely dangerous. You will have no control.
  › When you're riding on cold but dry roads and go underneath a bridge, be careful to look for ice that may have formed from dripping water. (Or if you're unsure, get off your bike and walk on the sidewalk under the bridge).
  › If you do hit ice, don't panic and don't brake. Once a bike stops quickly on ice, it will immediately slide because almost all the weight is over the rear wheel. You will hit the ground before you know it, *and a car may then hit you.*
› Keep your wits about you. Try not to squeeze the handlebars too hard or you may lose control of the front wheel. Keep a firm grip on the bars and stop pedaling. Stay as balanced as possible by keeping your feet on the pedals with the crank arm parallel to the road so your feet are across from each other. Allow the bike to coast over the ice.

6 Dress for the Ride

THE BASIC GEAR

Bottoms

Spandex cycling shorts have a seamless chamois crotch area, come in male and female designs, and should be long enough to cover most of your thigh. If you're touring for a few days, it's important to keep your cycling shorts clean or you may get a nasty infection. Always travel with two pairs – wash one pair at night and let it dry, tied to your panniers, while you wear the other. This lightweight but durable material dries quickly. For those who don't like spandex, there are lots of comfortable, baggier touring shorts to choose from. (For bottoms options in colder weather, see "Staying Warm.")

Tops

T-shirts are fine on nice-weather days, but because the cotton absorbs your sweat and stays wet, you'll need other options on chilly or rainy days (see "Staying Warm").

Cycling jerseys are made of quick-drying material, with pockets in the back for snacks. A rolled–up nylon rain jacket fits in too, which can save your life in changing weather. A reflective mesh vest is also a lifesaver, in case you get stuck in the dark. Choose brightly colored jerseys and jackets to improve your visibility.

Don't wear anything, top or bottom, that flaps around. Loose clothing gets caught in bikes, blocks your and others' sight lines, and will slow you down as it catches the wind (plus, you'll look like a sail). Stay compact.

If you're riding to a destination where you'll be a while, bring a change of clothes/clean underwear in a pannier or small backpack, especially on a hot day.

Chamois is great padding but incubates bacteria.

Feet
Don't ride without socks; wear ankle socks in summer. Your feet do a lot of work and will sweat; they need to be surrounded by an absorbent material.

Hands
Padded fingerless cycling gloves make a huge difference because of the body weight that rests on your hands. Gloves make cycling more comfortable, and should you crash, they protect hands from road rash (scrapes and little pieces of gravel embedded in your palms).

If you want to clean off your tires as you ride because you went through glass, you can reach down and rest your gloved hand on the tire as it rotates. Never do this with a bare hand!

Cycling gloves also make great nose wipes, so take them off before you shake someone's hand. Clean them often by wearing them while you wash your hands with lots of soap. Hang dry.

STAYING WARM
The biggest concern when riding in chilly temperatures is hypothermia. Your body temperature drops from the normal 98.6°F (37°C) to between 90°F and 95°F (32°C and 35°C), and your breathing, heart rate, and blood pressure all slow down. You start to lose coordination, may have intense shivers, rigid muscles, vision problems, and feel disoriented – which could lead to a serious bike accident.

If you see other riders become pale and hear their speech slur, find a dry, warm place, get them out of wet clothes, wrap blankets around them, and give them warm, non-alcoholic drinks as soon as possible. If you don't stop hypothermia at these temperatures, it quickly slides into moderate and severe hypothermia, which can cause death. Frostbite often accompanies these symptoms.

Riding in weather colder than 50°F (10°C) takes planning, beginning – and ending – at your feet. Between 39°F and 50°F (4°C and 10°C), wool or ski socks are perfect. Next, wear windpants with reflective strips. Then put on a long undershirt made of high-tech fibers or good ol' wool that wicks moisture from your skin.

Next, put on a fleece jacket, wool sweater, or fleece vest. They are excellent wicking fibers, and are cuddly and warm. Bring a lightweight jacket that keeps wind out and is water repellant, but don't wear it until you have to tackle a head-wind or it turns cooler. Make sure your jacket is a bright color and has reflective tape (same goes for your backpack).

If it's colder than 39°F (4°C), wear warm mitts. You won't get frostbite at this temperature, but if your hands become so cold you have trouble moving your fingers, squeezing the brakes could be a problem. Freezing hands are also painful.

A light balaclava under your helmet will keep your head warm, or you can loosen your helmet at the back and wear a headband. Only very thin toques fit under helmets properly. Finally, put your shoes on and tuck the laces in to avoid Laces Caught in Chain Syndrome, which suddenly throws you over the bars.

STAYING COOL

The biggest concern when riding in hot weather is hyperthermia: an increase in body temperature greater than the body's ability to cool itself. Hyperthermia will speed up heart rate, blood pressure, and breathing. Symptoms include weakness, nausea, fainting, dizziness, confusion, and stomach and muscle cramps. Skin may become cool and moist.

Get hyperthermic riders to lie down in the shade (or, ideally, air conditioning) and give them cool, non-alcoholic, and caffeine-free drinks. Sponge them with cool water. If you can't get indoors, run through sprinklers or use a garden hose to douse yourself and other cyclists. Find safe, clean swimming conditions and dive in; find a fountain, take your helmet off, and then soak your head completely, followed by your helmet and jersey. Refill all waterbottles, and do not start riding until everyone feels strong. Normally, hyperthermia is easily recovered from if the body returns to the right balance of heating up/cooling down. If this doesn't happen, the hyperthermic person could die.

A helmet with plenty of air vents protects your head from direct sunlight. When you add sunglasses, nearly all of your head is protected. You can also drape a bandana across your neck. Wear light colors, as they don't absorb heat.

Cycling in hot weather without drinking lots of water is very dangerous. Your body is mainly water, so refill often, stopping under shade for your breaks. Eating is also important, even if you don't feel like it. Juicy oranges, apples, and other easily carried fruits, including bananas, are perfect. Carry energy bars in your jersey pockets.

STAYING DRY

If you think it might rain, pack rainwear in your backpack or panniers. Some lightweight jackets fold into their own pocket and fit just about anywhere. Coated nylon will keep you drier longer than plain nylon (which works for about one minute). There are high-tech jackets made out of waterproof, breathable fabrics, but you are still growing and they are expensive.

When Mother Nature Throws a Curveball

You may have to improvise during sudden weather changes. If the temperature drops, place a folded section of newspaper inside the front of your jersey. If your chest and stomach are warm, the rest of your body won't cool down so quickly. Plastic and paper bags and paper towels work well too.

Cyclists also put bread bags over their socks for warm, dry feet. Make sure the bags are tucked tightly into the top of your socks so your chain doesn't catch them. Bread bags work for cold hands too. When I got caught in cold rain riding from Banff to Calgary, I stopped at a coffee shop and used the plastic packaging sleeves from take-out cups. They came to my elbows like evening gloves and over my legs like knee socks – I was elegant and dry!

THE BIRTH OF THE BLOOMER

Amelia Bloomer was the first woman in the United States to publish and edit a newspaper. *The Lilly* advocated, among other things, liberating clothing. Voluminous skirts and petticoats were useless on a bicycle. How could you straddle the saddle with such trappings on? It was a cousin of one of Amelia Bloomer's friends – Elizabeth Smith Miller – who invented the split-skirt pantaloons now called "bloomers." When Amelia Bloomer wrote of them in *The Lilly*, bloomers changed the lives of women.

Amelia Bloomer

ACCESSORIES

If you try to hold something while you also hold your handlebars, eventually whatever you're holding ends up in your front wheel and you'll fly over the bars. Avoid this by safely transporting extra gear.

For school and around town, a backpack is great. It goes wherever you go. There are excellent cycling backpacks that distribute weight evenly, so not all the weight zeroes in on one area. (Yeow!)

When cycling beyond school or the store, panniers (saddlebags) are the best choice. You'll need to attach a rear carrying rack for them. I love my shiny red, completely waterproof panniers. They have accompanied me on at least 6,200 miles (10,000 km) of exciting trips.

No matter where you're going, your gear should always include: a helmet, a pump, and a toolkit with a spare tube, patches, Allen (or hex) keys, and tire irons. These should always stay under your saddle, unless you think they may be stolen. For longer tours, you may want to add more tools.

COMMUTING TO SCHOOL OR FRIENDS:

☐ lock (Don't forget the key.)

☐ waterbottle

☐ bell

☐ backpack if you need it

A DAY TRIP:

☐ backpack, courier bag, or one pannier

☐ lunch and snacks

☐ waterbottle/camelback

☐ extra clothing if cool temperature

☐ lights, reflective vest if out after dark

☐ lock, bell

PEDALING THE PLANET

In 1884, American Thomas Stevens, having never ridden a bicycle, decided to cycle around the world on a high-wheel "ordinary" bike. He left San Francisco in the spring of 1884 and finished in Japan in June 1888. He cycled from the American west coast to the eastern seaboard, sailed to Germany, and continued to Austria, Eastern Europe, and into Turkey. From there he pedaled through the Middle East, Afghanistan, India, and China until he reached Japan. What makes his tale quite unbelievable is how little gear he packed: extra socks, one extra shirt, a slicker-raincoat, a bedroll, and a tent. He consumed whatever local water and food he could find. Eventually he carried a gun and became fiercer than some of the characters he encountered. In 1884, he wrote about his experiences for *Outing Magazine*, which shaped his book, *Around the World on a Bicycle*.

Thomas Stevens

A WEEKEND TRIP:

- ☐ panniers (Don't use a backpack for a day or more of riding; it's too much pressure on your back and crotch.)

- ☐ two waterbottles/one camelback

- ☐ rainwear (This keeps the wind out but is flammable – be careful near camp-fires.)

- ☐ extra pair of socks and cycling shorts

- ☐ T-shirt, fleece jacket, or vest (depending on weather. In warm weather, you can sleep in a T-shirt; for cool, cozy sleeps wear fleece.)

- ☐ if camping, bring essential camping gear (You have to carry this, so good-bye inflatable raft!)

- ☐ sleeping bag (smallest possible – limited room in panniers)

- ☐ first-aid kit (Completing a first-aid course is a good idea too.)

- ☐ food: lots of complex carbohydrates (pasta or rice, fruit, oatmeal cookies) and proteins (Be careful with meat, fish, or eggs – they go bad quickly and cause food poisoning if not stored properly.)

- ☐ lock (You don't want to wake up to a missing bike.)

- ☐ bell, lights

RACE DAY:

Make sure your bike is in good working order well before race day. Don't start tinkering with brake pads when you should be getting a good night's sleep before the race! In order to sleep with a calm mind, prepare the night before, including your lunch. Have everything at the front door in a backpack or duffle bag alongside your bike.

- ☐ DO NOT FORGET YOUR HELMET!

- ☐ cycling shoes/socks

- ☐ cycling shorts/clean regular shorts or pants, underwear

- ☐ cycling jersey

- ☐ cycling gloves

- ☐ sunglasses

- ☐ at least two waterbottles

- ☐ tools

- ☐ pump

- ☐ racing licence (if applicable)

- ☐ other clothes (weather dependent)

- ☐ easily digested lunch/snack food (bananas, oranges, raisins, granola bars, and some serious post-race food)

7 Bike Maintenance

Your bicycle is your best friend – don't ignore regular maintenance. The more you take care of it, the more it is worth as a trade-in when you've outgrown it. When considering a bike for trade in, bike shops will know in a glance whether you took care of your bike.

Keep your bike indoors. Not only is it unlikely to be stolen, but it will last many more years if it isn't exposed to snow and rain. Tires last longer when not always exposed to the sun's rays.

Build up your toolkit. Start with the necessities for under your saddle, but learn bike repairs from bike shops, clubs, or recreation centers. Many offer courses. Once you start fixing your own bike, you will need a truing stand (upside-down pair of old forks nailed to a platform and some chalk), pedal wrench, bottom-bracket remover, cone wrenches, headset tools, and a spoke key to start off. Check out local bike-shop mechanics – what do they use?

BEFORE AND AFTER EACH RIDE

Before you ride each day, check that the quick-release wheels (if you have them) are secured properly.

If your tires/tubes are lightweight, they will lose air – pump them up when they feel soft. If you hold your index finger to your thumb and flick against the tire, you should hear a *ping*, not a *pong*, for road riding. For off-road trails, a lower tire pressure is better for grip; keeping a diary of riding conditions will help determine pressure. Road or off-road, you want efficiency and safety. Tire pressure that is too low on road bikes causes the tube to be pinched by the tire and go flat; tire pressure too high on a mountain bike won't provide traction. The part of the bike that touches the earth – the tire – is a critical part of the cycling equation. Keep this relationship in mind.

Clean your bike after riding in rain, mud, sand, snow, construction sites, and dusty areas. Old toothbrushes are perfect for cleaning between chainlinks and behind sprockets and pulleys. Save everyone's old T-shirts or socks to use as terrific bike rags. Put your hand inside a sock to hold on to greasy, grimy parts.

Dry and clean the drivetrain immediately. This part of your bike will rust in minutes and become very inefficient. Cleaning doesn't take long, and you're already muddy. Why not get a little dirtier? After cleaning, lube the area and wipe off any excess.

WEEKLY MAINTENANCE

Brakes should be checked each week with the one-finger test. When you pull on your brake levers, you should only be able to fit one finger between the lever and the handlebars. The levers must snap back. If there is no snap or the levers touch the bar when they're pulled, get the brakes adjusted immediately.

Do the "drop test" weekly. Pick the bike up just an inch (2.5 cm) above the ground and drop it so it lands on the tires. Hear anything tinkling or rattling? If so, find out and make sure it is adjusted.

MONTHLY MAINTENANCE

Each month, or after really rugged rides, test all bearing placements. This means moving the crank arms, looking for sideways play from the bottom bracket, and moving both wheels to see if they have any sideways play (if they do, the bearings inside the cone in the hub must be attended to).

Finally, hold the handlebars so the front of the bike is off the ground. Gently rock the wheel back and forth. If it moves smoothly, the headset bearings are fine. If you feel tension, these bearings need to be adjusted.

SEASONAL MAINTENANCE

When you put your bike away for the season, take it in to a good bike shop (ideally, the one you bought it from) for an overhaul. Don't wait until March when everyone and their brother suddenly remember they need their bike fixed.

8 Feed Your Body, Fuel Your Bike

BIOMECHANICS

You now know about the mechanical brilliance of the bicycle. When *you* jump on your bike, it becomes a work of *bio-mechanical* brilliance. Your body is a complex collage of interconnected systems – fueled by calories and oxygen – constantly interacting with one another and the environment to produce you.

Stand straight with knees rigid – try to jump. Can't get off the ground? Bend your knees and jump again. This time you propel yourself upward. Why? The muscles you used to jump can't work properly unless the joint they also work with is engaged in the movement. Jump again. Your hips swing as your butt moves backward. Did you swing your arms too? This is bio-mechanics at work – bodies know how to jump efficiently and engage the right joints. Your central nervous system and muscle-skeletal system are involved in the execution of movement too – that's why you're a collage.

THE RIGHT BIKE SIZE

When bodies have biomechanical efficiency on a bicycle, the joints work with major muscles to propel the bicycle through a "cycle" that allows your skeletal system to bend at angles that bring the most power from cycling muscles. You can demonstrate this by trying to ride bikes that are too small or too big. Too-small bikes don't allow your leg muscles to extend to a length that allows them to be efficient pistons, which would occur if the hip and knee joints are bent at optimally efficient angles. The rest of your body's muscles can't do their job: to allow the most en-gaged muscles – those of the legs – to work either. You can't even keep your bal-ance and end up putting your foot down.

The opposite happens with a too-big bike. Leg muscles hyperextend in order to reach the pedals and the optimal angle your hips and knees need for efficient pedaling is not realized. Balance is lost not because your body is cramped up but because it's stretched too far.

THE RIGHT BIKE FUEL

You've probably heard this before: *You are what you eat.*

Imagine your food as gasoline; your body as the engine. Cars can't run on sugar water and neither can you. Nor can you run on too much fat. Bodies simply can't per-form on junk food. (Too much junk food harms your body, and who wants that?)

With the help of nutrition guides you can determine what is and isn't healthy food by reading the ingredients listed on packages. Treat yourself to ice cream, ham-burgers, or chips now and then – doctors say if you are eating well the rest of the time and getting lots of exercise, you can have fast food twice a week. Once you've had your fix, what might the rest of your diet look like if you are:

- riding your bike for more than an hour
- riding your bike to your soccer prac-tice/game and riding home
- riding to the beach, swimming/playing volleyball, and riding home?

Complex carbohydrates are the secret to being able to do all this and not get too tired.

Complex Carbohydrates

Cyclists need complex carbohydrates such as hot cereals (slow-cooking por-ridge) and non-sugared cereals (muesli) in the morning. Your body converts and then stores the complex carbohydrates found in these whole grains as glycogen (a type of sugar used as energy) in the muscles. The milk you add to your cereal is fortified with vitamin D and provides protein and calcium. Add some maple syrup, raisins, or honey. Bananas are great because they provide potassium, a mineral that helps transfer important information to your muscles and helps prevent cramping.

Sandwiches made with whole-grain and multi-grain breads are the perfect lunch for cyclists. If you want something sweet, choose fruit, oatmeal cookies, date squares, or muffins. Homemade sweets usually contain less sugar, fat, and chemicals than store-bought treats.

Cyclists are notorious pasta lovers. If you watch films about the Tour de France, when cyclists sit down to dinner, bowls brimming with pasta and perfectly done tomato sauce appear. We can't seem to get enough Italian food! These meals provide complex carbohydrates, especially with whole-wheat pasta. Brown and wild rice work well too.

Vitamins

The B vitamins, found in the breads and cereals already mentioned, help build a cyclist's body, while grapefruits, oranges, tomatoes, and apples provide vitamin C.

They contain water too, something a dehydrated body craves. You'll also find vitamin A and minerals in many other fruits and vegetables, particularly root vegetables, so eat plenty.

Protein and Iron

Don't neglect protein, which is found in meat, beans (including tofu), nuts, and dairy products. Protein is absolutely necessary for a growing body. Imagine it as your body's building blocks. You can eat plenty of protein without getting too much fat by not choosing deep-fried chicken or other fried meat. Eat peanut butter made only of peanuts, and read the ingredients label on all foods to avoid excess fat and sugar.

If you don't eat meat, make sure you eat enough iron, especially if you are female. A nutrition guide will help you determine the iron in food choices. It's essential in cycling and all aerobic sports because of the role it plays in delivering oxygen to muscles.

Calcium

Calcium is also crucial for cyclists. If protein is building blocks, calcium is the cement that helps the building blocks stand strong. While calcium works with all parts of our body, bones and teeth need a daily supply.

EATING WHILE CYCLING

Making your favorite food destination the last stop on your ride is a great treat. If you do this in the city, bring your lock – food can be very distracting. Or you can plan a ride with friends or family and cycle to a barbecue at someone's home or cottage or a picnic in the park. They supply the food; you supply the appetite.

There's nothing like a ride through the countryside when farmers are selling fresh fruits and vegetables at roadside stands. But don't count on finding enough roadside food to keep energy levels up. If you're riding for more than an hour, have food with you. Cyclists can get "the bonk," which means there are few energy reserves left in the body. Available glycogen has been used up. You need to quickly eat simple carbohydrates from sweets or fruits and lots of water if you start to feel sluggish and may not be able to see clearly. If you are in the middle of nowhere, this may not be possible, so always make sure you have food with you.

Pack food in your backpack or pannier. Chose your proteins carefully to avoid food poisoning in hot weather. Nuts and raisins are perfect, along with energy or granola bars. (Read the label, though, as many granola bars contain way too much fat.) Bring along fruit and eat the bananas first. They don't survive hot days. Cookies are great; muffins tend to get mushed.

DRINKING WHILE CYCLING

Never leave home without a full waterbottle. You can also use a camelback – a backpack with a strong plastic bag in it for water and a tube that allows you to drink without taking your hands off the handlebars. (Camelbacks are harder to clean, however; you don't want to start a science project in there.) If you know you're going for a long ride, fill waterbottles with juice or a mix of water and juice. Close your waterbottle properly each time you drink, as the road does not need your valuable fluids, you do.

Seventy percent of your body is made of water – even more when you are growing – and if you start dehydrating, it is essential that you replace the lost water immediately. If you're really active on a hot day, you can lose up to 10 percent of your bodyweight through dehydration, causing hyperthermia (see Chapter 6). If you are riding by yourself, you may not notice what is happening until it is too late. This is why riding with friends and family is always a good idea. Refill your waterbottle at gas stations, stores, houses, or restaurants – anywhere with clean water. Go to a house asking for water if you have to, but do this with friends to ensure safety. This is no time to be shy. You absolutely must have a good supply of water on longer rides.

Pros Take It Up a Gear

What if you loved cycling so much and were so good at it that it became your job? No, you didn't become a bike courier, though that's an option: you became a full-time bike racer.

Greg LeMond and Lance Armstrong put road racing on the map for North Americans by winning the Tour de France a combined ten times from 1986 to 2005. LeMond and Armstrong follow a legendary line-up of North American cyclists, such as American Connie Carpenter Phinney, the first woman to win a gold medal at the 1984 Olympics in Los Angeles (when women cyclists were finally allowed into the Games). Before her, Sheila Young won multiple World Sprint Champion gold medals on the velodrome (cycling track). Vancouver cyclist Alison Sydor won a bronze medal at the World Road Championships in 1991, then switched to mountain biking and has won more world cups, world championships, and top-five "podium finishes" than any other cyclist on the planet. She has competed in four Olympics, coming home with a silver medal in 1996.

There is a long and exciting history of cycling, but it is the legendary Tour de France that captivates us every summer. First held in 1903 with 78 riders cycling for eighteen days in July and for more than 1,500 miles (2,400 km) – through the stunning Pyrenees and Alps, French vineyards, the tiniest of villages, and the Champs-Élysées in Paris for the final sprint – the Tour de France was organized by Victor Goddet and Henri Desgrange. They wanted to create the biggest, hardest, most French bike race ever. Today the names of Fausto Coppi, Felice Gimondi, Eddy Merckx, Raymond Poullidor, Jacques Anquetil, Greg LeMond, and of course Lance Armstrong are synonymous with the Tour.

LANCE ARMSTRONG

How is it possible for someone to have cancer in the testicles, the lungs, the brain, with signs that it's invading more of the body, and not only recover but go on to win the world's toughest sporting event seven times straight? American cyclist Lance Armstrong is truly a legend. He utterly devastated the competition in each Tour de France, winning seven times in a row from 1999 to 2005.

Armstrong entered the international scene in 1993 when he won the world championships road race. He joined a European professional team and by 1996 was a strong and reliable racer. But that fall, after finding blood in his saliva, feeling overwhelmingly tired, and having pain in his testicles, he went to the doctor. Armstrong learned that the cancer was spreading and soon he was receiving the latest treatments, which made him terribly sick. He lost a year and a half from competitive cycling but rode his bike nearly every day while ill. When he returned to competi-

tive cycling in 1998, a reporter wrote, "Life, all of life, nothing but life" of Armstrong's resilient spirit.

The Armstrong monopoly of the Tour de France was called "the comeback of the century" and continued until 2005. During that time, North America fell in love with the Tour. People of all ages got into cycling and became dedicated to their own fitness. Armstrong retired after the Tour in 2005 and received a great show of respect and admiration from all of Europe as he stood triumphantly on the winner's podium on the Champs-Élysées. In 2009, he returned to competitive cycling, placing third in the Tour de France that year.

Lance Armstrong

BERYL BURTON

A time trial is a race where competitors race from the start line one at a time, usually every minute. They ride the same course and the same distance, and when all the riders are finished they find out who had the fastest time. It takes great concentration to stay so focused on riding hard. Time trials really hurt because they take an all-out effort, so people who can tolerate pain well have an advantage.

From 1959 to 1983, Beryl Burton won Britain's "Best All Rounder" title for her amazing time-trialing ability. She was the world champion in the road race in 1960 and 1967, the silver medalist in 1961, and

THE FIRST AFRICAN AMERICAN CYCLING CHAMPION

Just a few decades after slavery was abolished in the United States, Major Taylor, an African American cyclist originally from Indianapolis, became the American and world champion (1899, 1900, and 1901). He held many world records. While Taylor had certain supporters in the white community, he constantly faced angry white racers who would do anything to try to make him lose – even if it endangered his life. Despite their nasty behavior and interference, Taylor never retaliated. He just worked harder and got ahead so they couldn't catch him. After beating every U.S. racer, he signed a lucrative contract to race in France, which took him all over Europe, where he was hugely popular. Major Taylor was headline news for years and years.

Major Taylor

Beryl Burton

the 3,000-meter pursuit world champion in 1959, 1960, 1962, 1963, and 1966. She won the silver medal in the 1961, 1964, and 1968 world championships and the bronze in the 1967, 1970, and 1973 world championships. In 1974, when she represented Great Britain at the world championships, one of her teammates was her daughter! Unfortunately for Beryl and her contemporaries, women cyclists were not allowed into the Olympic Games until 1984, the Pan-Am Games until 1987, and the Commonwealth Games until 1990.

But even facing discrimination, Burton had incredible staying power. In 1967, she set a world record with 277.25 miles (446 km) covered in the twelve-hour event and bettered the men's record by 5.75 miles (9 km). When she passed the lead man, she dug into her pocket and gave him a candy. Despite being hit by cars many times and having many injuries, Burton continued to cycle until age fifty-nine, when she died of heart failure while riding her beloved bicycle.

FAUSTO COPPI

Italian Fausto Coppi dominated cycling in the late 1940s and 1950s and remains a national hero in Italy. He won the Giro d'Italia (Tour of Italy) in 1940 and 1947. In 1942, he set a new world record for the hour on the velodrome. He won the Tour de France in 1949, becoming the first cyclist to win the Tour, the Giro, and la Primavera – a famous one-day race from Milan to San Remo – all in the same year. La

Primavera (which means "springtime," as it is held in mid-March) is the longest one-day race at 183 miles (294 km). Coppi won the Tour again in 1952. Riding for the Bianchi team, he was a thin, wiry cyclist – a superb hill climber. Victor Goddet, one of the founders of the Tour, watched Coppi climb the legendary Alpe d'Huez switchbacks in the French Alps and wrote, "Coppi climbing is like a ski-lift gliding up on its steel cable."

GUNN RITA DAEHLE

Norway is best known for its cross-country skiers, but this cross-country mountain biker – Gunn Rita Daehle – has rewritten the record book.

Mountain biking became a sport at the Olympics in 1996, and it was eight years later in 2004 on a hot, dusty day at the Athens Olympics that Daehle gave Norway its first Olympic gold in cross-country mountain biking. This victory came after winning the world championships in 2003 and 2004. By that time, she had also won three world cup overall championships and three European championships. Daehle continued to dominate the women's field at the world championships after the Olympics by winning the 2004 and 2005 world titles too. In 2005, she won six of the seven world cup races and the first Marathon World Mountain Bike Championships.

Fausto Coppi

Gunn Rita Daehle

In 2008, she won her eighth gold medal at the world championships for the marathon race of 89 kilometers.

Daehle had bike problems at the 2008 Beijing Olympics and did not finish the race. She had a baby in March 2009 and came back to competitive racing in July of that year to win another international race.

CLARA HUGHES

Only four athletes in the history of the Olympics have won medals in both the summer and winter Olympics – and Canada's Clara Hughes is one of them.

Growing up in Winnipeg, Manitoba, Hughes started speed-skating as a teenager but was soon recruited to cycling. In her first year of cycling competition, she won the junior Canadian championships. She entered the senior category two years later and in 1993 represented Canada at the world championships, where she was fifth in the 3,000-meter pursuit. In 1994, she raced in the women's Tour de France and wore the leader's coveted yellow jersey for the first three days. By the end of the tour, Hughes and her teammates had placed second overall, behind the powerful Russian team. The next year she won a silver medal at the world championships in the time trial, and at the 1996 Atlanta Olympics, she broke away with two other riders and scooped the bronze in the road race. Nearly two weeks later, she took another bronze in the time trial.

Hughes longed for her skates, however,

Clara Hughes

and switched back to speed skating. At the 2002 Salt Lake City Olympics, she won the bronze in the 5,000 meter and four years later scooped the gold in the same event and added a silver in the team event at the Turin Winter Games. She covered the cycling events at the 2008 Beijing Olympics for CBC and continues to ride her bicycle when not skating, exploring the world, and talking to kids about every child's right to play.

EDDY MERCKX

Belgian racer Eddy Merckx was known as "the cannibal" for his ability to eat through packs of cyclists to win the Tour de France, the Giro d'Italia, other famous European tours, or any of the one-day "classic" races that stretched more than 125 miles (200 km) each. Merckx won his first amateur world championship title in 1964 and then turned pro. After winning the Giro d'Italia, Tour of Flanders, the one-day races of Fleche Wallonne, Paris-Robaix, three Milan-San Remos, and the professional world championship title, he devastated the competition in his first Tour in 1969. A reporter wrote: "His rhythmic pedaling at a constant speed . . . [is] in such harmony that the general elegance of his pace was not affected."

Merckx would win the Tour five times, something only three other cyclists

would be able to do until the arrival of American racer Lance Armstrong. It wasn't just Merckx's dominance in the Tour that made him the greatest cyclist ever to live. It was his complete dominance of every race he entered. In 2004 at the Athens Olympics, Merckx witnessed his son, Axel, win the bronze medal in the road race. The family continues to have a knack for riding a bike.

THE LAST MILE

I coach the Anishinaabe Racers – a mountain bike team (ages seven to fourteen) from Chippewa of Nawash First Nation in Ontario, Canada. Team members live on the west coast of Georgian Bay, about 25 miles (40 km) north of Wiarton and 120 miles (200 km) north of Toronto. When they ride through the woods today, they are riding the trails their ancestors used to hunt and snowshoe.

One team member, Shania Squires, learned how to ride when she was in kindergarten. "My bike had training wheels on it, and my mom told me to bike around with my sisters," says Shania. "I had butterflies. I thought I was going too fast. I fell and cut my knee, but my sister told me to get up or else go home. I fell again and biked home. When the cuts healed, I gave the bike another try. This time I felt happy."

When Shania was in grade one, her sisters tricked her. They took the training wheels off her bike, and when Shania got on it, they told her that they were holding her bike from behind but had really let go. All of a sudden Shania was balancing on two wheels. It was the start of an exceptional cycling career.

In 2006, Shania's friend Tamara asked her to join a mountain bike race. "I felt nervous when I got there, but when I was actually racing, I forgot about my nerves," says Shania, who placed second behind Tamara. The next year, Shania was the first girl across the finish line. "It felt cool," Shania says. "I was right behind the first boy."

In 2008, Shania entered her first Ontario Elementary School Mountain Bike Championships. "I wasn't really nervous, but I didn't know the track so I followed the girls ahead of me. I felt good in the race, like I was actually doing something helpful for myself."

Shania won the bronze medal. She says it felt scary going up to the podium because so many people were taking pictures. When she came home, she showed her grandmother her medal and says she felt proud. It was a magical day.

I hope the same magic happens for you.

INDEX